VERONA for TRAVELERS

-The total guide-

The comprehensive traveling guide for all your traveling needs.

© 2019 by THE TOTAL TRAVEL GUIDE COMPANY
© 2019 by BRENDA PUBLISHING
All rights reserved

PUBLISHED BY

THE TOTAL TRAVEL GUIDE COMPANY

TABLE OF CONTENTS

Why do we claim our guides are "total guides"?

Preface: Verona by Locals

Chapter 1: Why Come to Verona?

Chapter 2: Verona Local Travel Advice

Chapter 3: – Verona On A Budget

Chapter 4: Verona Travel Basics

Chapter 5: Transportation Options

Chapter 6: Best Hotels and Restaurants

Chapter 7: Verona's Cultural Opportunities

Chapter 8: Shopping Opportunities

Chapter 9: So Are You Coming Here?

PS: Please Leave Your Review

Why do we claim our guides are "total guides"?

Why are they really comprehensive?

Because we do almost anything to make sure that all the main issues relevant to the conscious traveler are covered in our guides.

We hate the typical boring travel guides chocked up with standard information you can readily find on the Internet.

We travel, we research other guides, we talk to locals, we ask friends, we ask friends of friends,

we do whatever it takes to make sure that we have you covered. All the angles! This is how we get the best tips, the most valuable for every one of our travel destinations.

That is where we got the best tips, the most valuable ones about our travel destinations.

All our guides are reviewed and edited by a "local" writer to make sure that the guide is one of its kind, comprehensive, fun and interesting. We prefer not to add too many maps or photos since you can have all that on the internet. We prefer to focus the content on tips and unique data that makes worthwhile to buy our total guides.

We use different approaches for each city, as each destination is unique. You will be able to verify that our guides are not standardized. Each one is different because each place is different. And you will enjoy the difference,

Our production team is very proud of our guides. We hope you will enjoy the reading and take full advantage of your traveling.   !

Preface: Verona by Locals

Verona (view from the hills) – Photo source: pixabay.com

Verona is one of the most popular destinations in the northern part of Italy, being visited by people from all over the world. A city of mystery, Verona is often chosen as a destination, as there are a lot of tourists who feel drawn to its artistic heritage. Regardless of the countries they come from, they want to see the ancient buildings that were built by Romans and to be part of the cultural events that are organized here on a regular basis. And, most importantly, they want to see the town that Shakespeare has presented in three of his most popular plays, including ever famous Romeo and Juliet.

If you decide to come to Verona, you are in for a real treat. You get to see a piece of Italy that could be easily compared to heaven. Every step you will take, you will discover that romance fills the air in Verona. This town is the perfect choice for a honeymoon, as it is more romantic than you can imagine. So, if you have just got married or you are looking to rekindle the lost flame of passion, you should definitely consider Verona for your next holiday. Use this book as your faithful guide for a pleasant travel, especially since it contains specific advice from locals living right there.

Start with the first chapter, in which you will discover the main reasons why you should consider coming to Verona. Move on slowly to the second chapter, in which you will discover specific advice from locals like myself. In this chapter, you will find information that is quite useful and not presented in the common travel guides you can purchase. Go the third chapter to find out how you can travel to Verona on a budget – this is particularly useful if you have chosen this destination but you are under a tight budget. Find out the things that are free or discounted in Verona, preparing for a holiday that is as fun as it is affordable.

The fourth chapter includes all the travel basics you might need for your trip to Verona, allowing you to remain efficient in the planning of the future holiday. The fifth chapter is dedicated to the transportation opportunities in Verona, which is highly useful for you as a tourist. Move on to the sixth chapter in which you will find presented the best hotels and restaurants of Verona. Surely, you will find something there to appeal to your interest.

The seventh chapter includes the most important cultural opportunities that Verona has to offer, demonstrating that this town is really a splendid choice from all points of view. As for the eighth chapter, this includes only information on the shopping choices you have available in Verona. If you are interested in shopping sprees, this is the right town for you to visit. The book concludes with a wonderful portrait of Verona, reminding you of the reasons that made you choose this city in the first place. Enjoy reading!

Chapter 1: Why Come to Verona?

Arena di Verona – Photo source: pixabay.com

To say that Verona is a romantic city would be the understatement of the century. Verona is the city of Shakespeare and it is quite famous for the romantic atmosphere, as it was already mentioned. And if you really want to experience romance at its finest, you need to come to Verona on Valentine's Day. Each year, Verona In Love Festival (http://www.veronainlove.it/en/) is organized in our amazing town, promoting the concept of love and romance through different music concerts, exhibitions of art and a wide range of other activities that you will simply adore.

The city is so filled with history, that you will have a wonderful time walking around the town and discovering the ancient buildings that have made Verona a part of the UNESCO World Heritage list. Surely, you will want to see the House of Juliet or Casa di Giulietta (Via Cappello, 23; +390458034303), as it is known in Italian. You can step inside the small courtyard and see what is supposed to have been the home of Juliet, depicted in the world-renowned play of Shakespeare, Romeo and Juliet. It is said that rubbing the statue of Juliet is going to bring you good luck, so do not hesitate to try it out. You can also take photos of the famous balcony on which Juliet awaited for her Romeo and post your own love note in the wall.

If you are interested in discovering a bit of the romantic Verona before you actually visit it, you can watch the 2010 movie Letters to Juliet. Apart from a wonderful interpretation from Amanda Seyfried, you can see her coming to the house of Juliet and discovering a love note that has been placed in the wall many years ago. Not many people know but Juliet's Club (depicted in the movie) really exists; they have responded to many love notes and ensured the continuing of a beautiful tradition (http://www.julietclub.com/en/). Once you arrive to Verona, you can also visit the inside of the house, which dates from the 13th Century. Inside, you will find a small museum but, the important thing is that you can actually step on the famous balcony and have your picture taken.

In case you are interested in discovering more about Romeo and Juliet, you can visit one of the local tourist offices. Here, you will be given information about how you can reach Casa di Romeo (Via delle Arche Scaligeri) and San Francesco al Corso Monastery (Via del Pontiere), where it is said that you can see the tomb of Juliet.

From Casa di Giulietta, you can go to the famous Piazza delle Erbe, an iconic landmark of the beautiful Verona. During the day, you can spend your time shopping for all sort of knick-knacks. However, the place comes alive during the evening, where you can see elegantly-dressed Italians sipping their wine and enjoying the sweet Italian life. You too can sit at a table and enjoy yourself just as much, being instantly reminded of why you love Italy.

The great thing about this piazza is that it allows tourists to admire some of the most interesting architectural jewels that Verona has to offer. Just a quick glance and you would already have come across the antique tower with its many steps, the fountain in which coins are thrown for good luck and the medieval palaces with their frescoes dating from centuries ago.

For someone who loves architecture, Verona is a splendid choice. You need to come to this town and discover the wonderful works of art that are found inside the medieval palace known as Castelvecchio (http://www.museodicastelvecchio.comune.verona.it/; Corso Castelvecchio 2; +390458062611). You will admire the exterior architecture of this wonderful old castle and also the works of artists such as Canaletto, Tintoretto and Titian on the inside. The visit to Verona should also include Basilica di San Zeno Maggiore (http://www.basilicasanzeno.it/; Piazza San Zeno 2; +390458006120), built in the elegant Romanesque style and adorned with intricate details made from bronze. And you would be remiss if you wouldn't visit Palazzo di Cangrande or Palazzo degli Scaligeri (Piazza dei Signori), as it is also known. This was once the home of the Scaligeri family, who ruled Verona around the 13th Century.

It is said that the best way to see Verona's beautiful buildings is to climb the 368 steps of the antique tower. From the top of the Torre dei Lamberti (Via della Costa 1; +390459273027), you can see a splendid overview of the town and even Austria, provided there are no clouds in the sky. The tower is 275 feet high but if you feel like you are not up for the stairs challenge, you can always take the elevator.

Culture should also represent a strong reason why you should come to Verona. This city has always maintained a reputation for being a capital of culture and, upon arriving here, you cannot help but be seduced by the endless cultural opportunities. The art scene is filled with events of the highest possible quality, always organized in a sublime and quite romantic setting. During your stay, you can enjoy amazing productions of ballet and opera at the famous Teatro Filarmonico (Via dei Mutilati 4; +390458002275).

Perhaps one of the most interesting experiences that should draw you to Verona would be the possibility to see a play of Shakespeare or to listen to a jazz concert in the world-renowned Arena di Verona (http://www.arena.it/en/; Piazza Bra 28; +390458005151). With approximately 15000 seats, this is one of the best preserved Roman amphitheaters in the entire Italy and definitely a feast for the eyes. During the months of summer, an opera festival is organized here, drawing millions of tourists who are looking to discover elegant productions. They all want to sit in the same place where Romans used to sit, cheering for the gladiators they admired.

Verona is also a great city to visit for a shopping indulgence, presenting an impressive selection whereas such matters are concerned. As you will see in the chapter dedicated to the shopping opportunities of Verona, there are luxury brands that present the latest creations but also retailers that sell vintage items at really affordable prices. It is recommended that you check out the Italian fashion while sitting at a restaurant terrace, with a good bottle of wine and a traditional delicious meal (however, if you are not too crazy about horse meat, be sure to avoid the things that have caval, the Italian world for horse). You can also go to Via Mazzini and check out Italians strolling, dressed in the latest, most fashionable clothing. This is a ritual for the people from Italy, being known as the passeggiata.

Chapter 2: Verona Local Travel Advice

Juliet's Balcony – Photo source: pixabay.com

As someone living in Verona, I can tell you that this town is pretty amazing. You have so many opportunities here as a tourist, that you will not even feel when the time has passed. I definitely recommend visiting Verona during the period of the carnival – this is an event with a tradition that goes back 600 years and it is more beautiful than you can imagine. Allow yourself to be pleasantly impressed with the Veronese carnival masks and enjoy the local parades. The carnival is organized with two weeks before the traditional Christmas lent period.

The accommodation in Verona should depend on how you long you are planning on staying here and also on the kind of person you are. If you are staying for a couple of days and you like to listen to the bustling crowd, you should definitely consider a hotel or a lovely B&B in the center. On the other hand, if you have decided to spend a longer period of time in Verona and you want some peace and quiet, I can recommend that you rent something in Valdonega. This district is located up on the Veronese hills and you have some splendid views from there.

Depending on the amount of time you have to spend in Verona, I strongly urge you to take a day trip in the nearby areas. Verona has a lot to offer as a city but you can set one day aside and go to the beautiful Lake Garda, which is located at a close distance. You can get lost in small, Italian villages such as Bardolino, Garda or Malcesine, discovering the local culture and the friendly people who welcome tourists from all over the world. If you want a unique experience, I recommended that you take a one-day trip to one of the vineyards in the area, such as Soave, Valpolicella or Recioto. Here, you have the opportunity to taste a delicious glass of wine and enjoy the true flavor of Italian living. As for those who are amateur photographs, I can say that the village of Borghetto is totally worth visiting, as it has a beautiful watermill (approximate distance from Verona – 35 km). Spend at least one week in Verona to get a taste of it; otherwise, you will feel like you have traveled here for a quick sprint.

Us, Veronese, we are very proud of our local dishes, considering them to be a feast for both the eyes and the mouth. If you come to Verona, make sure that you try out the local dishes, such as the famous risotto with its different dressings and side salads, the products that are made from horse meat (it doesn't get more local than that) and the polenta dishes that are often adorned with delicious cheese or mushroom toppings. And if you are a fan of fish, there are plenty of dishes that you can try out, with subtle herbs bringing out their flavor.

In Italy, and especially in Verona, no meal is complete without a sweet dessert. While in Verona, I recommend that you try out Juliet's kisses (baci di Giulietta), small chocolate cookies with toasted almonds, the traditional sponge cake that is eaten around Christmas (Pandoro of Verona), zaletti biscuits made from cornmeal and the Veronese chestnut flour cake known as Castagnaccio. It is said that food connects you with the culture of a people and the traditional Veronese dishes do not make an exception from this rule.

As this is the town of Romeo and Juliet, you will definitely visit the House of Juliet and leave your own love card or message in the famous wall. However, I must advise you against using gum in order to attach the love card to the walls. Keep in mind that this is a historic building that dates from the 13th century and it is quite impolite to leave your gum there.

If you want to befriend the locals of Verona, like myself, all you have to do is go to the Piazza delle Erbe in the evening. There are plenty of restaurants and bars here, with beautiful terraces and we, Italians, love nothing more than to sit down to a meal or a glass of wine, talking with new and exciting people. As for the language, you might discover that we prefer speaking in the local, Veronese dialect of Italian; however, given the fact that this town is visited by an impressive number of tourists, we also speak English and German. So, you do not have to worry about language barriers, as these are easily overcome with a good bottle of wine. In the morning, however, you can enjoy a delicious Italian espresso, while reading a newspaper or listening to the locals discussing about sports.

Not surprisingly, both the locals and the tourists coming to Verona adore the ice cream from here. The famous gelato has the most unique texture, with interesting flavors such as fig and pear being offered in certain places. If you have always wanted to try this frozen indulgence, there is no better location than Verona to do that.

While Piazza delle Erbe is one of the most famous touristic points of interest in Verona, I also recommend visiting the nearby Piazza dei Signori. This is a smaller piazza, but it is certainly quieter, as there are far less tourists here. However, I like it because of the Italian charm it exudes. Plus, at a close distance from Piazza dei Signori, you can find the Centro Internazionale di Fotografia Scavi Scaligeri (http://www.scaviscaligeri.comune.verona.it/; Cortile del Tribunale; +390458007490), where amazing photographic exhibitions are taken among historic Roman ruins.

As I have mentioned in the previous chapter, the summer in Verona is dedicated to the famous Opera Festival. If you are interested in coming to this part of Italy during that period, I recommend that you book your hotel in advance. You need to do such a thing because of two very important reasons: on one hand, the prices for the hotel rooms tend to sky rocket during the opera festival and, on the other hand, you can expect not to be able to find rooms, as the city is flooded with tourists.

If you go to the famous Roman amphitheater, do not hesitate to go all the way to the top and enjoy the amazing view of Verona from there. On Sunday, if you want to bond with the local culture, you can go to the church and attend mass. I recommend the San Lorenzo Church (Corso Cavour 28; +390458050000), as the beautiful building dates from the 8th Century and the simple decorated interior promotes a feeling of peace and quiet. The church can also be visited in the afternoon, for those who are not interested in attending mass.

As you can see, Verona is a town of multiple facets. You can enjoy a delicious and typical brunch, visit the beautiful Giardino Giusti (Via Giardino Giusti 2; +390458034029) in the famous Veronetta district and rent a bike to see the rest of Verona. It is all about creating memories that you are going to cherish for life.

Chapter 3: – Verona On A Budget

Roman Theatre (remains) – Photo source: Pixabay.com

If you are coming to Verona and you do not have too much money to spend, I can recommend that you purchase the Verona Card. For those of you who have traveled to other European cities, you are probably accustomed with this type of purchase. This tourist card has the advantage of offering you a free one-time entrance to the most important cultural attractions that Verona has to offer, whether we are talking about museums, churches or other cultural monuments. The Verona Card is available for 24 hours (€18 price) or for 48 hours (€22 price).

The biggest advantage of the Verona Card is that you do not have to worry about entrance fees anymore; instead of calculating how much money you still have left and other things like that, you can really enjoy the things you are visiting with the cumulative ticket. Among the attractions that are included in the Verona Card, you will find the following: GAM (Modern Art Gallery), Centro Internazionale di Fotografia Scavi Scaligeri, Old Radios Museum, San Fermo Maggiore Church, Duomo of Verona, Sant'Anastasia Church, San Zeno Church, Natural History Museum,

Castelvecchio and Museum, Lapidary Inscriptions Museum, Roman Theatre, Juliet's Tomb and Frescoes Museum, Juliet's House, Lamberti Tower and Arena. As you can see, you have quite a long list of attractions that you can see for the affordable prices mentioned above.

There is one more thing that you should know about the Verona Card. Apart from the free entry offered to the main points of attractions, you can also use it for discounted tickets at the following: Sala Boggian (part of the Castelvecchio Museum), Miniscalchi Erizzo Museum, Arena Museo Opera, African Museum and Giardino Giusti. And, as all the other European tourist cards, this particular one comes with free transportation (bus) for the duration of the card.

The Verona Card becomes valid the moment you use it in order to visit a museum or other points of attraction. It can also become valid if you use it for the purpose of public transportation. As you have read in the first paragraph, there are two possibilities of purchase for the Verona Card. There are no special categories for students or the elderly but you have to remember that the majority of the tourist attractions have their own discounts. On the plus side, kids who are under the age of 7 are commonly granted free entry to the tourist attractions that Verona has to offer.

Where can you buy the Verona Card? First of all, you can go to the different tourist offices that are located in different parts of Verona. You can also find it at tobacco shops or at the different points of attractions, including in museums, churches or different other monuments. You can always decide to purchase the Verona Card and use it at a later date; as it was already said, it becomes valid only when used.

Apart from the Verona Card, you can also decide to purchase a cumulative ticket and see the churches in the town. All the churches in Verona have gathered in an association and it is possible to see all of them by paying the discounted price of €5 (keep in mind that a single-admission costs €2.5, so the cumulative ticket is definitely more advantageous). The cumulative ticket grants admission to the following churches: Sant'Anastasia, San Fermo, San Zeno and the Duomo. For someone who is passionate about religion and churches, this ticket is the ideal choice. If that is not the case of you, the Verona Card is a more suitable alternative.

Walking through the streets of Verona is also recommended, as it does not cost anything. You can see the wonderful architecture, discovering the beautiful Cathedral of Verona (http://www.cattedralediverona.it/; Piazza Duomo 21; +39045592813) that was built in a splendid mixture of Gothic and Romanesque styles, the San Zeno Church and Porta Borsari. Porta Borsari is an ancient Roman gate, representing the old entrance into Verona (from the southern part) and it is amazing to see how beautifully this ancient ruin has integrated into the modern city of today.

I would also like to let you in on another secret. As a local living in Verona, I can tell you that, in the first Sunday of every month, you can see for free the following tourist attractions: Juliet's Tomb, Roman Theatre and Castelvecchio Museum. Another free thing that you can enjoy while walking in Verona is represented by Arco della Costa, which is a giant whalebone hanging from an arch in the famous Piazza delle Erbe. The whalebone was placed in this location more than 1000 years ago, after having been dug up from the area and as a suggestion that Verona was once under water. There is even a legend behind this – as it is said that the whalebone will fall on the first person who has never told a lie.

As you can see, it is possible to come to Verona, even when you are on a tight budget. You can enjoy the free entries with the affordable Verona Card and you can simply walk through town, feasting your eyes on the amazing architecture. This is indeed the kind of city that can suit everyone's preferences, regardless of the available budget. And, yes, it is possible to create memories without having to pay a fortune for them.

Chapter 4: Verona Travel Basics

Piazza Citadella – Photo source: Pixabay.com

Verona is one of the most popular tourist destinations of northern Italy, being part of the Veneto region (country code is 39 and the one of Verona is 045). In order to have a fantastic trip to Verona, there are a few things you need to take into consideration. Read the information presented in this chapter and organize your to-do list before going away.

First and foremost, if you want to travel to Verona, you should know that there are several opportunities. You can choose to travel by plane, arriving on the Verona Villafranca Airport, which is located at approximately 12 km from the center of the town. Both budget airlines and national carriers arrive on the airport of Verona, coming from major European cities, such as: Moscow, Rome, London, Paris, Munich, Frankfurt, Madrid, Dublin and Brussels. You can also arrive on one of the two Venetian airports, these being one hour away from Verona.

From the airport, you can use the shuttle bus service, as this will take you straight to the main railway station of Verona (Verona Porta Nuova). The railway station is located at a walking distance from the city center, so you do not have to worry about using other methods of transportation. The price for a single-ticket journey is of €6 and the journey between the airport and the railway station lasts for approximately 20 minutes. The shuttle bus service is available between 6 am and 11 pm every day, the buses coming at 15 minutes apart. You can purchase the tickets for the shuttle bus service from the special machines that are located at the airport bus stop or directly from the driver.

If you want, you can travel to Verona by car, using the motorway in order to reach the city. The railway system functions to perfection, providing three main categories of trains to potential travelers: regional, high speed and international. The Italian railway system, Trenitalia, can be used in order to travel to Verona from other cities of the country, such as: Belzano, Trieste, Rome, Florence, Bologna, Turin, Venice and Milan. International trains can be used by those coming to Verona from other countries of Europe, including Austria, Germany, France and Switzerland. And if you really want a unique experience, you should definitely try out the luxury tourist train. This passes through Verona, having the following route: Venice-London-Innsbruck-Paris.

In deciding on Verona for your next holiday, you should be aware that, coming outside Europe, you will need a valid passport in order to enter the territory of Italy. If you are coming from one of the countries that are members of the European Union, all you need for your travel is the ID card (no visa or passport required).

I should also warn you that the majority of the tourist attractions in Verona are closed on Mondays. Given such matters, you can use this day in order to take a trip to the beautiful Lake Garda or spend the day walking on the cobblestone streets of the city, discovering one elegant piazza after the other.

In general, Verona is a relatively safe city, with a low rate of crime. The one thing you have to be on the lookout for is pickpockets. These are especially found in the areas where there are many tourists and they are quite agile when it comes to stealing your wallet or slicing through your purse. Protect yourself from pickpockets by wearing a small purse under your garments and never keep your wallet in the back pocket. As for the ladies, avoid carrying your purse on the shoulder and do not walk around town wearing expensive jewelry (you will attract the attention of the wrong kind of people). Among the areas that you should be careful, there are: Portoni della Bra (historic city gate), Verona's historic center, the entrance to the Arena (Roman amphitheater) and Via Mazzani.

As you will have the opportunity to discover, a large part of Verona's historic center is pedestrianized. Avoid driving around these parts and especially around the Arena, as you will surely get a ticket. Watch out for the pedestrian only signs, as these are a clear indication that no vehicles are allowed. On the other hand, if you are a pedestrian, you have to be extra careful when crossing the street. This is because Italian drivers are not that attentive and they do not always stop at the crosswalks. Clearly, we cannot present this as a general rule for all the drivers in Verona, but it is for the best that you are careful and look twice before crossing the street.

Being part of the European Union, the currency in Verona (as in the rest of Italy) is euro. If you need to exchange money, it is recommended that you choose a bank rather than a cash exchange office. If you do have to use a cash exchange office, make sure that you check out the commission taken for each transaction. Some cash exchange offices present their commission in a very small print, so you might miss it if you do not pay attention to such details and end up losing a part of your money through that transaction.

In case you are wondering when is the best time to visit Verona (in terms of weather), I can recommend that you arrive here either at the end of spring or at the start of autumn. There are far less tourists here and you can enjoy both the peaceful cobblestone streets and the reduced prices for different types of accommodation. If you prefer Verona in the winter, you can come here between November and February, with a suitcase of warm clothes. The good news is that you can go skiing in the nearby areas, enjoying the winter sports to the fullest. If you prefer the summer, you can come to Verona but I must warn you about the high temperatures and the excess humidity. For those of you who can handle such kind of weather, summer is the perfect choice to see the attractions of Verona.

These are the basics things you should know before traveling to Verona. It might help you to go through the chapter again and, as I said at the start, organize a list with everything you need for the perfect holiday.

Chapter 5: Transportation Options

Verona Lane – Photo source: Pixabay.com

If you find yourself in the center of Verona, chances are you will not need to use public transportation, as everything here is within walking distance. However, the bus service is recommended for those who want to reach further districts of Verona or they have chosen a hotel in the suburbs.

The main bus station is located right in front of the main train station and it allows you to take the bus and reach different neighborhoods of Verona, as well as Lake

Garda. The majority of the buses are orange in color but you will also find buses that are green and black or blue and grey. The schedule of the buses, as well as a map of the entire bus service, can be found on the website of the bus company ATV (http://www.atv.verona.it). Keep in mind that Verona has now one single company for bus transportation; in the past, there were two companies, one providing buses for the city transportation (Urbani – city buses) and the other one handling transportation outside Verona (Extraurbani – out-of-town buses).

It is recommended that you buy the tickets for the transportation before you get on the bus. Surely, you can buy them onboard but these are commonly sold at a higher price and it would be a shame to waste your money (+ €0.80 extra charge). Also, do not forget to validate your ticket the moment you have stepped on the bus. The bus service functions very well and there are plenty of stops throughout the entire city. Just keep in mind that the bus service functions by a different timetable when there are holidays, on Sunday and during the night.

There are approximately 20 bus routes that can be used for transportation in Verona. If you want to save money on transportation, you can buy a day pass – this will give you unlimited travel time with the Veronese buses. Do not forget that the Verona Card also offers free transportation for the period it is valid.

Apart from the special shuttle line between Verona and the airport, during the summer, you can use the bus and travel to Lake Garda. You will have the opportunity to discover the beautiful Riviera degli Ulivi; moreover, you can travel with the bus from Garda to other towns in the area, such as Bardolino, Lazise and Peschiera. The bus lines have been especially organized, so as to connect the area of Lake Garda with the beautiful villages on the lakefront.

Holiday tickets can be purchased by tourists, for both the city buses and the out-of-town buses. The prices of the tickets vary accordingly to their duration: for the 1 day pass you will have to pay €13; the 3-day pass costs around €27 and the one for a week is about €49. During the summer, these are the special lines made available not only to tourists, but also to locals, like myself: Verona-Cattolica (takes you straight to the sea); Spiazzi – Madonna della Corona (you can travel from Lake Garda directly to the sanctuary); Bus 'Walk and Ride' (special bus line for those who are passionate about mountain biking); Lake Garda - Venice (you will need to book ahead for that); Arena di Verona – Lake Garda (bus line available during the Opera festival).

The taxi service can be useful for transportation in Verona – you can find taxis at the main train station or in Piazza Bra. Keep in mind that it is not customary for taxis to be hailed from the side of the road; even if you do that, they will not stop.

For trips outside Verona, you can use the railway system with all the confidence. The trains can take you anywhere you desire in Italy. The main train station is

Verona Porta Nuova and you can purchase tickets for the desired journeys from there (booking tickets in advance is also a good idea, allowing you to make sure that there are seats available. The one thing you have to remember is that, before you get on the train, you validate the ticket. There are special yellow machines on the platform, where you can validate your ticket. If you forget to do that, the ticket will not be valid and you will have to pay for another ticket on the train (at a higher price). There is a small chance that the person checking for the tickets is understanding but you have to let them know as soon as you have gotten on the train. You could end up paying a small fine but it is still better than having to pay for the ticket all over again.

Verona also has an excellent coach service, allowing tourists to reach other destinations on the Adriatic Coast or go to the ever popular Venice. You can use the coach service in order to travel to the destinations in the Veronese or Trento mountains. The most important thing is that the coach service is also accessible to passengers with disabilities, allowing those with impaired mobility to travel in comfort.

If you want to see the outskirts of Verona at your own pace, you can consider a car hire service. While there are plenty of car rental services in Verona, the best prices are to be found online, especially if you book the vehicle ahead of your holiday. However, you must keep in mind that car rentals are recommended only for longer journeys, outside Verona; in the town, and especially in the center, the car is not so useful and there are many pedestrianized areas where cars are not allowed.

Chapter 6: Best Hotels and Restaurants

Verona Adige River view – Photo source: pixabay.com

Finding the best hotels and restaurants in Verona might seem like a daunting task, as there are so many opportunities around. In order to facilitate the actual choosing of a hotel, I have selected ten of the finest hotels in Verona. As for the restaurants, these are ten in number as well. Do not hesitate to try all of them out, as each has some pretty interesting choices to offer in terms of cuisine.

These are 10 of the finest hotels in Verona:

1. Il Sogno Di Giulietta

o   Romantic setting

o   Located in a beautiful, medieval palazzo

o   Some of the rooms overlook Juliet's balcony

- 16 rooms available
- Antique furnishing, with bed frames that have intricate ornamentation and duvets with gold threads
- Stay in the same hotel with the actors from the famous movie 'Letters to Juliet'
- Sign the guestbook and see all the couples who have become engaged during their romantic stay
- Address: Via Cappello 23
- Tel.: +390458009932
- Website: http://www.sognodigiulietta.it/

2. Corte delle Pigne

- B&B style hotel
- Walking distance from Piazza delle Erbe
- Beautiful colors for each room
- Romantic elements – bed frame made from wrought iron, armoires inspired from the French style
- Breakfast in bed
- Small bar
- Address: Via Pigna 6
- Tel.: +393337584141
- Website: http://www.cortedellepigne.it/

3. Hotel Gabbia d'Oro

- Elegant and charming hotel
- Close to Porta dei Borsari and Piazza delle Erbe
- Located in a building dating from the 16th Century, covered in ivy
- Antique-style rooms
- Bright colors

- o   Unique elements of décor
- o   Address: Corso Porta Borsari 4
- o   Tel.: +390458003060
- o   Website: http://www.hotelgabbiadoro.it/

4. Relais Ristori

- o   Romantic-style hotel
- o   Elegant rooms decorated with antique furniture and beautiful, white linen
- o   Lovely courtyard
- o   Walking distance from Castelvecchio and Theatre Ristori
- o   You can stay in a room that has been named after historic lovers
- o   Address: Vicoletto Circolo 1
- o   Tel.: +390458673032
- o   Website: http://www.relaisristori.it/

5. Palazzo Victoria

- o   Luxury hotel
- o   Elegant bedrooms and suites
- o   Modern gadgets
- o   Private Jacuzzi
- o   White leather furniture
- o   Marble column and parquet floors
- o   Frescoes
- o   Excellent restaurant
- o   Close to the historic centre
- o   Address: Via Adua 8
- o   Tel.: +39045590566
- o   Website: http://www.palazzovictoria.com/

6. Byblos Art Hotel Villa Amista

- o   Boutique-style hotel
- o   Decorated with elegant, baroque furniture
- o   Beautiful landscaped gardens
- o   Contemporary art display in each room
- o   Elegant Venetian chandeliers dangle from the ceiling
- o   Excellent restaurant and spa
- o   Uniquely designed interior
- o   Address: Via Cedrare 78, Corrubbio di Negarine
- o   Tel.: +390456855555
- o   Website: http://www.byblosarthotel.com/

7. Delser

- o   Historic hotel
- o   Located outside Verona
- o   Free parking
- o   Rooms overlook the city
- o   Close to the train station
- o   Parquet floors and modern interior design
- o   Breakfast in the room
- o   Address: Dei Monti 14B
- o   Tel.: +390458011098
- o   Website: http://www.delserverona.com/

8. Le Suite Di Giulietta

- o   Romantic rooms
- o   Overlook Juliet's balcony

- o   Eco-friendly suites
- o   Located in a building dating from the 15th Century
- o   Close to Piazza delle Erbe
- o   Blend between modern and classic
- o   Breakfast served in the room (Italian-style)
- o   Address: Via Crocioni
- o   Tel.: +393272068209
- o   Website: http://suitedigiulietta.it/

9. Escalus Luxury Suites
- o   Close to Arena and Piazza Bra
- o   Modern and comfortable rooms
- o   Internet access
- o   Located on an important shopping artery
- o   Reception always open
- o   Newspaper offered to guests
- o   Breakfast in the room
- o   Address: Vicolo Tre Marchetti 12
- o   Tel.: +390458036754
- o   Website: http://www.escalusverona/com/

10. Due Torri Hotel
- o   Luxury hotel
- o   Elegant rooms
- o   Close to Church of St Anastasia and Juliet's balcony
- o   Comfortable and spacious suites
- o   Free Wi-Fi
- o   Cultural events organized in the hotel lobby

- o   Art Nouveau restaurant and bar
- o   Modern meeting rooms
- o   Address: Piazza Sant'Anastasia 4
- o   Tel.: +39045595044
- o   Website: http://www.duetorri.hotelsinverona.com/.

These are 10 of the best restaurants in Verona:

1. Al Pompiere

- o   Close to Juliet's House
- o   Trilingual menu
- o   Intimate atmosphere
- o   Recommended choices – specialty meats (prosciutto crudo), pasta, risotto
- o   Interesting and diverse wine selection (over 300 wines)
- o   Address: Vicolo Regina d'Ungheria 5
- o   Tel.: +390458030537
- o   Website: http://www.alpompiere.com

2. La Fontanina

- o   Elegant and romantic atmosphere
- o   Michelin-starred restaurant
- o   Close to the Arena
- o   200 years-old tradition
- o   Recommended choices – venison carpaccio, foie gras terrine, squid-ink pasta with fresh seafood
- o   Tasting menu offers a complete experience
- o   Address: Portichetti Fontanelle 3
- o   Tel.: +39045913305
- o   Website: http://www.ristorantelafontanina.com/

3. Osteria Sottoriva

- Servizio lente – no quick meals to be expected
- Ravishing dishes are served
- Recommended choices – braised tripe, gorgonzola melted over polenta, crepes with ricotta and spinach
- Generous portions
- Affordable prices
- Address: Via Sottoriva 9/a
- Tel.: +390458014323
- Website: http://www.sottorivaitalia.com/

4. Hosteria La Vecchia Fontanina

- Traditional Veronese cuisine
- Reasonable prices
- Talented chef (Marco Segattini)
- Only fresh produce used for the food
- Sunny outdoor terrace in the summer
- Recommended choices – pasta, risotto, gnocchi
- Excellent wine selection
- Address: Piazzetta Chiavica 5
- Tel.: +39045591159
- Website: http://www.ristorantevecchiafontanina.com/

5. Trattoria Papa e Cicia

- Located on the bank of Adige river
- Ten minutes away from the city center
- Classic Italian dishes

- o   Recommended choices – pasta, risotto
- o   Address: Via Seminario 4
- o   Tel.: +390458008384

6. Enocibus

- o   Close to Piazza Bra
- o   No fixed menus for lunch/dinner
- o   Friendly owners
- o   Recommended choices – pasta, salads, roasted pork
- o   Extensive wine list
- o   Address: Vicolo Pomo d'Oro 3
- o   Tel.: +39045594010
- o   Website: http://www.enocibus.com

7. Osteria Carroarmato

- o   One of the oldest osteries in Verona
- o   Extensive wine selection
- o   Opportunity to blend in with locals (long tables)
- o   Recommended choices – pasta and bean soup, polenta with melted cheese and mushrooms
- o   Address: Vicolo Gatto 2
- o   Tel.: +390458030175
- o   Website: http://www.carroarmato.it/

8. Osteria Al Duca

- o   Traditional cuisine
- o   Reasonable prices
- o   Close to Juliet's House

- o   Recommended choices – spaghetti with anchovies, veal with tuna and mayonnaise
- o   Address: Via Arche Scaligere 2
- o   Tel.: +39045594474

9. Tutt'Art

- o   Located in the San Nazaro district, close to the Giusti Gardens
- o   Italian cuisine, with Asian and Brazilian influences
- o   Recommended choices (gourmet menu) – roasted pork, cold pea soup, tropical fruit granita
- o   Address: Via San Nazaro 27
- o   Tel.: +390458030632
- o   Website: http://www.tuttart.com/

10. Vini Zampiera Alla Mandola

- o   Close to the Arena
- o   Wine bar – extensive selection of organic and natural wines
- o   Recommended food choices – local sausage, ham, cheese, pasta
- o   Address: Via Alberto Mario 23
- o   Tel.: +39045597053.

Do not forget to try out the recommended choices for the restaurants mentioned above and be sure to ask indications for a suitable bottle of wine to go with the food. After all, no Italian meal is complete without a good bottle of wine. And, as it is said, 'when in Rome, do as the Romans do'!

Chapter 7: Verona's Cultural Opportunities

Verona Theatre – Photo source: pixabay.com

There is always something happening in Verona, regardless of the season or the weather. If you like to visit towns for their cultural opportunities, you should know that Verona will match your every expectation in terms of culture. Let's check out some of the most important cultural highlights that this town has to offer.

Verona in Love is one of the most important festivals that takes place in this lovely Italian town, being completely dedicated to those who are in love. During this festival, you will discover a series of cultural events also taking place in the squares of the city. It is said that this festival is actually a tribute to San Valentine but also to the tragic love story of Romeo and Juliet. During the festival, tourists have the opportunity to listen to live music, taste the local cuisine and purchase all sorts of trinkets from the local markets. You will surely enjoy the discounted admission ticket to Juliet's house, the flying heart fireworks and the Romeo & Juliet half marathon (more information at http://www.veronainlove.it).

If you are a fan of music, you will surely want to visit Verona between July and September, listening to the wonderful concerts organized under the International Opera Festival. Held at the Arena and with a tradition of over 100 years, this festival is going to enrich your soul. Among the most interesting operas you will have the opportunity to see, there are: Carmina Burana, Il Barbiere di Siviglia, Don Giovanni, Tosca, Nabucco, Romeo et Juliet, Aida. Imagine how beautiful the Arena will looking, welcoming artists and tourists from all over the world (http://www.arena-verona.com/).

Music aficionados are invited to Verona during the period of the Verona Jazz Festival. This is organized in July, welcoming both national and international Jazz musicians. The events are organized in different locations of Verona, including the Arena, Corte Merchato Vecchio and Teatro Romano. You can obtain more information about this even by visiting http://www.veronalive.it/.

I personally like the Verona Summer Theatre Season, organized in the months of July and August, in the old Roman theatre. Tourists flock in to see the events that are included in this unique form of art – in July, you have the opportunity to see dramatic works, while the month of August is reserved for dance shows. You should also know that you will be seeing the works of Shakespeare and see dance shows with a Brazilian inspiration. More information about the Verona Summer Theatre Season can be found online, at http://www.estateteatraleveronese.it/).

Tocati is another traditional festival of Verona, being organized in the month of September, just at the start of autumn. This street festival has as main purpose the preservation of traditional games. Held in the historic center of Verona, it is a feast for the eyes. You can see both children and adults engaged in traditional games, spinning tops, using slings and clinking marbles. For the Tocati festival, the organizers invite a different country each year, guaranteeing the international diversity of this event. Apart from the games played on the street, you will surely enjoy the diversity of musical concerts, art exhibits and other cultural activities organized during the period of the festival. More information can be obtained online at http://www.tocati.it/.

The Feast of Santa Lucia is a very interesting event organized in December. In fact, the event takes place precisely on 13th of December, making the end of the winter solstice and also celebrating the reappearance of the sun in the northern hemisphere. With the occasion of this event, the Christmas market is opened in Piazza Bra and both tourists and local residents, like myself, have the opportunity to buy delicious traditional food and different trinkets that can be offered as gifts for Christmas.

If you come to Verona in March, just before the Lent period, you can see the Carnival of Verona. As it was mentioned in another chapter, this is one of oldest carnivals of Italy, with a tradition dating since the middle ages. There are lots of parties and cultural activities during the period of the carnival but the main point of attraction is the traditional parade. Over 4000 people take part in the parade, each wearing a masked costume. You will definitely have a lot of fun taking a look at the floats, hearing to the music of the brass bands and seeing the drum majorettes cheer.

There are over 500 floats taking part in the parade, with over 15.000 kg of sweets being thrown to the people on the side of the road. There is also a night parade, known as Carnevale di Notte a Monteforte, being held on the last Saturday of the carnival period. There are just as many floats and people wearing masked costumes as during the day events and you will surely enjoy the unique experience. You can see for yourself the information for next year's event at http://www.carnevalediverona.it.

The Festa del Cimbri a Camposilvano is organized on the first Sunday of July, being the kind of event that you never forget. There are all sorts of parades organized, not to mention religious rites and feasts. The tromboni shootings make this event even more unique and interesting to be a part of. The trombonis are actually ancient weapons, bearing an uncanny resemblance to the harquebus. Organized by the Curatorium Cimbricum Veronese, this event also crowns a king of the festival. Who knows? You might have come to Verona and end up becoming a king, even if it is just for one day.

During the autumn and more specifically in the second Sunday of September, you can take part in the Festa dell'Uva. This is actually a festival that celebrates grapes and the coming of autumn. If you want to feel like a local and blend in, you will take part in the different grape-featuring competitions and learn how to crush grapes with your feet.

As you have seen for yourself, Verona has a lot to offer in terms of culture. To conclude, I must remind you of the lovely film festival that takes place between March and April and of the big wine festival that is known all over the world (Vinitaly) with its wine tasting opportunities. Coming to Verona, you will definitely have a full visiting agenda. You will feel like there is so little time, given the fact that there are so many wonderful things to be seen and so many events to attend. I want to give you one single piece of advice: do not hurry to do everything. It is far better to see less but remain with more. A hurried holiday in Verona will leave you with a fade taste of what Italy is actually about – slow pace of life, good food and wine, history and culture.

Chapter 8: Shopping Opportunities

Flea market – Photo source: pixabay.com

As the other great cities of Italy, Verona has a lot of opportunities to offer in terms of shopping. Whether you are interested in visiting the flea markets that are organized on a regular basis or you are more attracted to the shops selling designer clothes, it is guaranteed that you will something to purchase. Italians have a passion for shopping – this I can tell you from my own experience. However, after a few days spent in Verona, you will become addicted to shopping as well. Let's find out more information on the subject.

Flea markets are quite popular among tourists and locals like myself, as they present a wide diversity of products. If you are patient and you look with attention to every product, you might find something quite extraordinary. For example, you might be able to purchase an old gramophone that still functions. Another big

43

advantage of the flea markets is that you can negotiate for the products you want to purchase. In fact, haggling for the final price is half the fun of the shopping experience.

In autumn, for every Sunday, a very nice antiques market is organized in Piazza San Zeno. You should not hesitate to visit this open-air market, as you will have the opportunity to see and purchase both antique furniture and paintings. There is also a daily market which is organized in Piazza delle Erbe – from here, you can purchase fresh fruits and vegetables, not to mention the most amazing selection of specific Italian herbs. You can also purchase clothes and shoes at discounted prices. And if you really like flea markets, you have to check out the one that is organized on the football stadium each and every Saturday.

If flea markets are not exactly your thing, you can visit the shopping arteries of Verona, such as the famous Via Mazzini. On this street, you will find stores that sell world-renowned, luxury brands, clearly at corresponding prices. Among the most popular brands that you will find here, there are: D&G, MaxMara, Fendi and Benneton. You probably already know that these products are on sale twice a year – once at the end of August/beginning of September for the summer collection and once at the end of December/beginning of January for the winter collection. Depending on your budget, you can purchase a wide array of products from the shops located on Via Mazzini, including exclusive handbags from popular designers and leather shoes that bear a characteristic signature. Other products include scarves from top quality silk and elegant suits that are tailor made.

Via Mazzini is not the only artery in which you can find such shops. As a matter of fact, all of Verona is filled with great shops, presenting the most incredible variety of products. You can check out the shops on Corso Portoni Borsari or the ones from Via Roma or Via Cappello. In the near vicinity of Piazza delle Erbe you will also find a great selection of shops. You can purchase clothes in the latest fashion, shoes to match your new outfit, a fragrance perfume that is delicate and souvenirs for your loved ones. The FNAC stores are located throughout the entire Verona, being the perfect choice for those who are interested in digital equipment, smartphones, books, computer games and other similar products. You can find such a store on Via Cappello 34, at a close distance from Juliet's Balcony.

For those of you who prefer shopping malls, Grande Mela Shopping Land is an excellent choice (http://www.lagrandemela.it). You will have to drive outside Verona, reaching the shopping mall after 8-10 km, on the road that normally takes you to Brescia. Here, you will find a huge array of products, distributed on no less than three floors. Apart from shops, you can also find a splendid selection of restaurants and cinemas presenting the latest movies. If you are interested in shopping for food and other similar products, you can visit the Auchan supermarket that is located at a close distance from the shopping mall.

Le Corti Venete is another shopping mall that you can decide to visit during your stay in Verona. It is found at the entrance of highway that takes you to the western part of Verona, presenting a wide array of shops as well. You should also keep in mind that the shopping malls are not open on Sundays, an exception from this rule being made only during the holiday season. Other from that, shopping malls are opened from 9 am to 8 pm. If you are looking to do some shopping but you cannot stand a lot of people, it might be for the best to visit the shopping malls during the week. These are very crowded on Friday afternoons and especially Saturdays, as everyone comes to the mall.

As opposed to the shopping malls, the shops that are found in the center of Verona are not closed on Sundays. However, you should know that Italians always take a lunch break, which means that the majority of the shops are not open during lunch hours (Italian siesta can last between 12.30 and 15.00 pm). Also, there are a lot of shops that are closed on Monday mornings, for inventory purposes.

In conclusion, Verona is an amazing city for those who are passionate about shopping. Coming to Verona, you will certainly leave with a baggage full of souvenirs, printed T-shirts and all sort of knick-knacks purchased from the flea markets. Depending on your budget, you can purchase designer clothing and accessories from luxury brands, feeling like you own the world. Perhaps you will fall in love with the elegant scarves that are sold in the little boutiques in the historic center or you will find the time to visit the discount designer outlets that are located outside Verona. Or maybe you will want to purchase a pair of top quality leather shoes (everyone knows that Verona is renowned for the leather tradition).

Chapter 9: So Are You Coming Here?

Verona by night – Photo source: Pixabay.com

Verona will forever remain as the town in which Romeo and Juliet have lived their tragic tale of love. People are always going to come to Verona and expect the town to offer romance above all else. Well, Verona successfully meets the expectations of tourists from all over the world – everywhere one looks, it seems as if romance fills the air. It is enough to watch the movie 'Letters to Juliet' once and you will instantly pack your bags and go to Verona. You will walk shyly into the courtyard of Juliet, see Juliet's balcony and see the wall in which romantic notes and love cards are still placed today, as they were centuries ago.

Couples can have the perfect holiday in Verona. Apart from the romanticism imposed by Shakespeare's tragedy, this town is filled with opportunities for history and culture. There are many buildings to be visited, with the Roman amphitheater being among the most popular. Apart from that, Verona has an amazingly rich calendar of cultural events, with a festival dedicated especially to the subject of love and the carnival that has a long tradition. You cannot get bored in Verona and, most importantly, you will have a great time while becoming involved in all sorts of activities.

Verona also offers a feast in terms of Italian cuisine. Everyone knows that Italian food is sensuous and delicious, bringing all your senses to life. Rich cheeses, mouth-watering specialty meats and fresh seafood are used as appetizers. Home-made traditional pasta, risotto and gnocchi are blended with fresh vegetables and meat/seafood for the most delicious meals you have ever tasted in your life. Chocolate desserts, always combined with the elegant vanilla gelato, will make you feel like you have died and gone to heaven.

Wine is to be enjoyed in Verona. Every restaurant or bar that you will visit in Verona will offer a splendid selection of wines. You can enjoy a good glass of wine with the above mentioned meals and the waiter will certainly take time in order to make the suitable recommendations. The wine will be chosen according to the type of meal you are serving but also on the age and other similar factors. If you are not a connoisseur of wine, you will certainly become one after some time spent in Verona.

Verona is the kind of city that makes you feel not young, but eternal. It makes you feel grateful for having lived to see and experience all of the things you are experiencing. It makes you think about the tragic love story of Romeo and Juliet and perhaps appreciate your partner more. It brings out the relaxed side in you, helping you discover the beauty of Italian living. The good food, paired with an excellent bottle of wine, might add on a few extra pounds but you will be so happy, that you will understand there are more important things in life. You will treasure Verona for having given you so much, despite being just one of the million tourists visiting this splendid part of Italy.

PS: PLEASE LEAVE YOUR REVIEW

If you reached this last page, probably this travel guide has given you some ideas about your stay in Verona!

Would you be kind enough to leave a review for this book on Amazon? It will help other travelers to find their way through this beautiful city!

Many thanks and enjoy your trip!

Copyright 2019 - All rights reserved.

This document is geared towards providing exact and reliable information in regards to the topic and issue covered. The publication is sold with the idea that the publisher is not required to render accounting, officially permitted, or otherwise, qualified services. If advice is necessary, legal or professional, a practiced individual in the profession should be ordered.

From a Declaration of Principles which was accepted and approved equally by a Committee of the American Bar Association and a Committee of Publishers and Associations.

In no way is it legal to reproduce, duplicate, or transmit any part of this document in either electronic means or in printed format. Recording of this publication is strictly prohibited and any storage of this document is not allowed unless with written permission from the publisher. All rights reserved.

The information provided herein is stated to be truthful and consistent, in that any liability, in terms of inattention or otherwise, by any usage or abuse of any policies, processes, or directions contained within is the solitary and utter responsibility of the recipient reader. Under no circumstances will any legal responsibility or blame be held against the publisher for any reparation, damages, or monetary loss due to the information herein, either directly or indirectly.

Respective authors own all copyrights not held by the publisher.

The information herein is offered for informational purposes solely, and is universal as so. The presentation of the information is without contract or any type of guarantee assurance.

The trademarks that are used are without any consent, and the publication of the trademark is without permission or backing by the trademark owner. All trademarks and brands within this book are for clarifying purposes only and are the owned by the owners themselves, not affiliated with this document.

THE END

Printed in Great Britain
by Amazon